ASTON VILLA

SECOND EDITION

This edition published by Carlton Books in 2012
First published by Carlton Books 2005

A CIP catalogue record for this book is available
from the British Library.

ISBN 978-1-84732-938-7

Printed in China

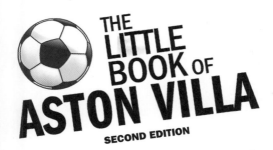

THE LITTLE BOOK OF
ASTON VILLA

SECOND EDITION

Edited by **DAVE WOODHALL**

CARLTON
BOOKS

INTRODUCTION

The history of Aston Villa bears striking similarities to the history of English football itself.

We gave the modern game to the world in the shape of the Football League, dominated in its formative years and then sat back complacently as everyone else went shooting past us.

There was a brief moment of glory some time ago when we proved that we could still compete with, and beat, all-comers but since then flattering to deceive has become an art form.

Contained herein are just a few of the many memorable statements made about the Villa. They combine to form an insight into the most historical, and infuriating, football club in the world.

66 If there is a club in the country which deserves to be dubbed the greatest, few will deny the right of Aston Villa to share the highest niche of fame with even the most historic of other aspirants. For brilliance and for consistency of achievement, for astute management and for general alertness, the superiors of Aston Villa cannot be found. **99**

William McGregor, Aston Villa committee member and founder of the Football League

" Since it has been our lot to frequent football matches we have never been witness of such disgraceful scenes. If the dribbling game is to be marred by such cowardly exhibitions, the sooner football is consigned to oblivion the better for all concerned. **"**

Birmingham's *Saturday News* on disturbances at the Villa v Preston FA Cup tie in 1888 when the cavalry were called in to restore order

" Every year it is becoming more and more difficult for football clubs of any standing to meet their friendly engagements and even arrange friendly matches. **"**

The opening sentence of the letter written by **William McGregor** to 11 other chairmen, which eventually led to the formation of the Football League, 1888

> **STOLEN!** From the Shop Window of W. Shilcock, Football Outfitter, Newtown Row, Birmingham, between the hour of 9-30 p.m. on Wednesday, the 11th September, and 7-30 a.m., on Thursday, the 12th inst., the ENGLISH CUP, the property of Aston Villa F.C.

Police poster after the original FA Cup was stolen while in Villa's care in 1895. The trophy was never recovered

66 I cannot judge the finer points of the game, but I can judge the great qualities displayed; those qualities distinctly recognized as British. **99**

Lord Rosebery on presenting Villa with the FA Cup in 1897

66 What pleasure could ladies ever have in watching a game of football on such a miserable afternoon? Would they not have been better employed at home darning socks or assisting in the housework rather than catching colds at Perry Barr? 99

The Birmingham Mail with less tact in 1896 than now

66 We like to get young men and train them into our particular style. This style is difficult to describe, but we prefer skilful control of the ball, sound defence and, above all, teamwork. **99**

Howard Spencer, turn-of-the-century Villa full-back, captain and later director

❝ Beware of the clever, sharp men who are creeping into the game. **❞**

William McGregor in *League Football and the Men Who Made It*, 1909

66 Finance is important, but we should never forget that we are not talking about a mere business. This is the Aston Villa football club, and it deserves nothing short of the best. 99

Club director **Frederick Rinder** during the boardroom battles of the 1920s

66 He earned the name because of his malodorous feet. **99**

Tranmere Rovers historian **Gilbert Upton** on how Tranmere and Villa legend Thomas 'Pongo' Waring came by his nickname

66 When Villa appoint a manager I hope the board will permit him to manage, and support him. 99

Sports Argus editorial on the club's decision to appoint their first manager in May 1934

> **The trouble with touring abroad with England is that everyone you meet only wants to talk about Aston Villa.**

Ted Drake, Arsenal and England centre-forward, in the 1930s

" In the very first minute of the match I went tumbling and landed flat on my face. The Villa fans howled with laughter, but I think it fair to say I had the last laugh. **"**

Ted Drake on the game in which he scored seven goals at Villa Park, December 1935

66 A civic, if not a national, disaster... **99**

The Birmingham Mail's editorial column after Villa
were first relegated in 1936

66 The Villa club has traditions second to none; above all, the material I have to work on possesses hereditary football ability. **99**

Villa manager **Jimmy Hogan** on his appointment in 1936

> **"** I've no time for those theories. Get the ball in the bloody net, that's what I want. **"**

Villa chairman **Frederick Normansell** at the time Hogan was appointed

" A great man in every way. "

Matt Busby's tribute to Jimmy Hogan upon the former Villa manager's death in 1974

66 They said we'd got to, so we said that for peace and quietness we'd give the Nazi salute. At the next place both teams gave the Nazi salute so we went to the centre of the field and gave them two fingers and they cheered like mad. **99**

Eric Houghton describes the furore surrounding Villa's 1938 tour of Nazi Germany when they were advised by the Foreign Office to follow local custom, and did so after a fashion

66 Training was terribly slack. Players strolled up at any old time. Some would just walk round the track and one used to go over the far side for a smoke. **99**

Peter McParland, scorer in the 1957 FA Cup Final, describes life at Villa Park in the 1950s

66 I suppose they'll let me pin the team sheet up this week. **99**

Villa manager **Alex Massie**'s reported comment to player Frank Moss during his reign in the late-1940s

66 Next stop –
Hall of Memories. **99**

Birmingham bus conductor, announcing his
vehicle's imminent arrival at Villa Park in the
mid-1950s

❝ I played with Ron in about a hundred reserve games. And, according to Ron, he was Man of the Match in at least 99 of them. **❞**

Former Villa player **Dennis Jackson** on his contemporary Ron Atkinson

66 He invented the banana shot. Trouble was, he was trying to shoot straight. **99**

Ron Atkinson returns the compliment with regard to Jackson's shooting abilities

66 As you got near to Villa Park, it was as if there was an army on the march. All you could see was people wearing Villa hats and scarves, carrying rattles and walking towards the ground. **99**

Entertainer **Allan Randall** on Villa in the 1950s

❝ Congratulations, Mercer. You've done it again. **❞**

A **Sheffield United supporter**'s telegram after Joe Mercer had led the Villa to relegation in 1959, two years after he had been manager of United when they were relegated

" The big myth of British soccer – that Aston Villa are still a major force. **"**

The Birmingham Post's sorry comment on the Villa Park situation, 1964

" They were lovely men, but they were totally unsuited to running a club like the Villa. They were too old, football was changing and they weren't up to it. **"**

Ex-manager **Tommy Cummings** pinpoints the reason for the Villa's failings in the 1960s. It was the directors…

❝ I told the manager, "If you keep buying Third Division players, where do you think you'll end up?" **❞**

Ex-Villa player and broadcaster **Larry Canning** on Villa's slide during the 1960s

> **❝** By now I would be as crazed with anticipation as was humanly possible without actually wetting myself. Villa Park was in sight, yet I could only reach it as fast as my legs could carry me. An hour to kick-off! Don't start without me! **❞**

Author **Simon Inglis** recalls his sense of anticipation on the way to Villa Park as a boy

> "There was something about it all that made an instant impression. It just hit me. I went home thinking, "I hope I get an opportunity to join that football club.""

Brian Little on the time he first visited Villa Park as a 15-year-old hopeful

❝ I went to the annual dinner of Walmley Cricket Club and, after suffering the usual abuse and derision, I thought, "This is not good enough." **❞**

Brian Evans on how he was inspired to lead the supporters' revolt which brought about the overthrow of the Villa board in 1968

66 I am sure that influential people in Birmingham, the sort of people who controlled things, decided a change was needed. They couldn't be seen to be involved publicly, but their influence was there. 99

Eric Woodward, who became Villa commercial manager, commenting on events that led to the board's mass resignation in 1968

66 Aston Villa will play in the European Cup one day. **99**

Tommy Docherty's prophetic parting shot after his dismissal as manager, January 1970

" When the visiting team went out to look at the pitch at two o'clock, there would already be more people in the ground than they were used to seeing at kick-off time. **"**

Former captain **Brian Godfrey** on Villa's prodigious Third Division crowds in the 1970s

66 Every good team has a strong centre. I'd look round. Goalkeeper, Jim Cumbes. I'd think, "What time did you get in last night?" Centre-half, Chris Nicholl. In the toilet putting his contact lenses in. Central midfield, Bruce Rioch. Shaking like a leaf. Centre-forward, Sammy Morgan. Next to Chris putting his contact lenses in. What chance did I have? **99**

Vic Crowe, Villa manager of the early 1970s

" We were playing away and we'd taken this 15-year-old apprentice with us. As was the custom, a whisky bottle was passed round. Players took a drink, then when they'd gone onto the pitch Vic Crowe took a big swig. The apprentice asked him why and he replied, "Son, when you're manager of this club you'll know why." **"**

Jim Cumbes, goalkeeper in the early 1970s

" I hopped in the taxi to Glasgow Airport with one thought in my mind – where on earth was Aston Villa? **"**

Andy Gray describes the journey that led to him signing for Villa in 1975

I got the impression that he didn't much like football.

Jim Cumbes on Ron Saunders, Villa's most successful-ever manager. He was in power from 1974 to 1982

" With 110% from each and every one of the players and your usual tremendous vocal backing, I am sure we can get the right result. **"**

Ron Saunders' programme notes invariably contained this or a similarly rousing phrase

"EVEN GRECIAN 2000 CAN'T STOP GRAY."

A supporter's banner at the 1977 League Cup Final, which finished 0–0. Villa won the cup after a second replay when Gray was absent

66 We often played golf together and he always beat me, then one day I won for the first time. Two weeks later, I was sold. **99**

Then club captain **Chris Nicholl** on why Ron Saunders offloaded him during the summer of 1977

> **My team won't freeze in the white heat of Anfield.** 🙲

Ron Saunders true to form as ever

66 I defy any football devotee not to sense that this would be a perfect setting for the championship trophy. **99**

The Evening Mail's **Ray Matts**, standing on the Villa Park pitch on the eve of the 1980–81 season

"He made me captain by saying, "Right, you lead 'em out."

Dennis Mortimer on how he was chosen by Ron Saunders to become Villa's most successful captain of all time

66 Does anyone want to bet against us...? Thank you for your confidence, gentlemen. **99**

Ron Saunders, after Villa were beaten in a vital championship decider against Ipswich in April 1981

" Let me be the first to congratulate Aston Villa. **"**

Radio Two announcer **Bryon Butler** as results elsewhere meant that Villa became league champions, May 1981

" I had more women than I scored goals. And I scored 23 goals. **"**

Gary Shaw on the 1980–81 Championship-winning season

> **There's a battle going on, but I am not leaving this football club.**

Ron Saunders to Dennis Mortimer, the day before his resignation in February 1982

❝My mum won't half be pleased.❞

Goalkeeper **Nigel Spink** to manager Tony Barton, as he was getting stripped to take Jimmy Rimmer's place after eight minutes of the 1982 European Cup final

> **Goal of the Season? No chance. Goal of the Month? Not a hope. It was only Goal of the Game because there were no others.**

Local journalist **Rob Bishop** on Peter Withe's European Cup winner in his book, *The Road to Rotterdam*

66 This is the shin that won the
European Cup. **99**

Peter Withe, rolling up his trouser leg in front
of celebrating Villa fans at the subsequent
civic reception

" The hardest part of captaining that team was tossing the coin and picking up the trophies. **"**

Dennis Mortimer, League Championship- and European Cup-winning captain

> **When you've been given a free transfer by Southport and Barrow, you learn to live with disappointment.**

Peter Withe after being dropped from the England squad in 1982

" The club will not accept constant failure. "

Chairman **Doug Ellis** on his reasons for sacking
Tony Barton for finishing 10th in 1983–84. Three
years later, Villa were relegated...

" Would anyone argue against the assertion that the Trinity Road entrance of Villa Park has more pomp and style than that of any other ground? "

Simon Inglis in *The Football Grounds of England and Wales*

> "Was that the season when you came home one night and said you were never going there again, even if they sent a chauffeur-driven limousine to collect you?"
>
> "Yes."
>
> "Then you went there the next Saturday?"

A conversation between Villa supporter **Peter Aldridge** and his wife recorded in *Heroes & Villains* fanzine

66 The whole club needs restructuring. The youth policy is not good enough, the scouting system is not good enough, the team is a shambles and I have come to sort it out. **99**

Graham Taylor upon his appointment as Villa manager in the summer of 1987

" You don't get this at Birmingham City. **"**

Doug Ellis prior to a recital by violin virtuoso
Nigel Kennedy at the Villa AGM

66 A swarming mass of humanity: 20,000 or more voices screaming out their support for the claret and blue. **99**

Villa fan **Simon Page** describes the pre-Taylor Report Holte End

> **You got yourselves into this f*****g mess. You can get yourselves out of it.**

Graham Taylor, when Villa were 2–0 down at half-time in an FA Cup third-round game at Crewe, January 1989. He then walked out of the dressing room. Villa won 3–2…

"We've signed enough injury-prone has-beens."

Anonymous **Villa supporter** quoted in the
Wolverhampton Express & Star when the club
bought Paul McGrath in 1989

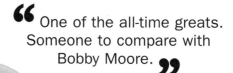

“ One of the all-time greats. Someone to compare with Bobby Moore. **”**

Jack Charlton on McGrath

" It is named after Paul McGrath, the best footballer in the world. **"**

The owner of the Irish pub McGrath's in Copenhagen, explaining the reasoning behind its name

" Twenty-seven years old, choice health, good knees, world-class agent. There was no way I could fail. **"**

Tony Cascarino describes his record-breaking move to Villa in 1990

> **I am a human being. I support Aston Villa, but I am still a human being.**

John Taylor, prospective Conservative parliamentary candidate for Cheltenham, after being racially abused by fellow Tories, 1990

“ FOR GOD'S SAKE GO DOCTOR JO... ”

The Evening Mail, reacting to defeat in time-honoured fashion by calling for the dismissal of manager Dr Josef Venglos, April 1991

" If he'd come a few years later he might have done better because by then the European ideas were better accepted... English football was always going to go the European way and Jo was the start of it. **"**

Former Villa midfielder **Paul Birch** offers a different slant on Venglos' time at Villa Park

If that lad makes a First Division footballer, then I'm Mao Tse Tung.

Tommy Docherty on Dwight Yorke after his Villa debut in 1990. Eight years later he was sold to Manchester United for £12.6 million

66 I'll never be able to achieve what Tommy Docherty did and take Aston Villa into the Third Division and Manchester United into the Second Division. 99

Ron Atkinson

> Someone asked me last week if I miss the Villa. I said, "No, I live in one."

David Platt after his record-breaking transfer to Bari, 1991

> **"** As a youngster I was one of Villa's keenest supporters. I played there and I always believed that one day I would return as manager. **"**

Ron Atkinson

> **"** I just wanted to give them some technical advice. I told them the game had started. **"**

Ron Atkinson explaining why he moved from the stand to the dug-out during a game with Sheffield United, 1993

66 People in this game don't realise how lucky they are. You drive to the ground, play a few five-a-sides, then have lunch. It's wonderful, enjoyable fun. **99**

Atkinson again, speaking when Villa were pushing for the Premiership title, 1993

> **"** I always make sure I write "Atkinson, D." on the team-sheet. Sometimes I wonder if I'm making a mistake. **"**

Ron Atkinson on the inconsistencies of his namesake, Dalian

" It's nice that Terry (Cooper) has his son playing for us and you've got your son here. "

Blues chief executive **Karren Brady**, getting her Atkinsons mixed up

❝ Once Tony Daley opens his legs, you're in trouble. **❞**

Former Leeds manager **Howard Wilkinson**

**" When you walk,
through a storm... "**

Villa compere **Dave Chance**, leading the community
singing of "You'll Never Walk Alone" before the
Holte End's last game, in 1994, against Liverpool.
The rest of the song was lost in boos and jeers

> **"What was your highlight of the tournament?"**
> **"Bumping into Frank Sinatra."**

Ron Atkinson quizzed by a journalist following the 1994 World Cup, after he had been criticised by Villa supporters for neglecting his managerial duties

66 You wouldn't have done that if Eamonn Deacy was playing. **99**

Voice from the Holte End as Ruud Gullit strode majestically through the Villa defence for Chelsea, 1996. Former Villa defender Deacy was not known for his cultured approach to the beautiful game...

" Why didn't you just belt it? **"**

Barbara Southgate after her lad Gareth missed
that penalty in Euro 96

" Our shares are a good bet in the short, medium and long term. "

Villa finance director **Mark Ansell** after the club floated on the Stock Exchange in 1997, with shares at £11 each. Five years later they were trading at just over £1

“ The game has been tailored to the wine-bar fraternity. The culture has gradually been eradicated. **”**

Classical violinist and Villa supporter
Nigel Kennedy, 1997

" This is my field of dreams. **"**

Stan Collymore on Villa Park pitch
after signing in May 1997

> **Stan's a lovely man, a lovely lad. He's just made one or two bad decisions.**

Brian Little on his record signing, and nemesis, Mr Collymore

66 How does Stan Collymore change a light bulb? He holds it in the air and the world revolves around it. **99**

Joke doing the Villa Park rounds during another of Collymore's absences

66 We knew how close we were to being a real force, but the more we tried to make that leap, the further away we seemed to be. Alex Ferguson said Villa was the team he could see coming through. **99**

Gareth Southgate on Villa's maddeningly close brush with the elite under Brian Little

" I'd like to play for an Italian club, like Barcelona... **"**

Mark Draper, who later joined English club Southampton

" I would not sign for another club, not even for 15 million dollars. However, it would be different if they were to instead offer me 15 different women from all around the world. I would tell the club chairman: "Please let me make these women happy – I will satisfy them like they have never been satisfied before." **"**

Sasa Curcic has his own way of asking for a transfer

66 The accelerator's position meant my right knee was giving me grief. **99**

Diminutive full-back **Alan Wright**, explaining why he was selling his £50,000 Ferrari, 1997

"You're merde, and you know you are."

Villa supporters during a UEFA Cup match in Bordeaux, 1997

66 We spent enough money, we just bought the wrong players. **99**

Former assistant manager, **Allan Evans**, explaining Villa's fall from grace during 1997–98

> ## If I'd had a gun I'd have shot him.

John Gregory after Dwight Yorke informed his manager that he wanted to leave Villa for Manchester United, August 1998

“ The chairman of Brighton wouldn't recognize Gareth Barry if he was stood on Brighton beach in the team strip, with a seagull on his head and a ball in his hand. **”**

Gregory in response to claims that Brighton made Barry the player he is and were worthy of a £2.5m compensation payment

> **"** There's an aura about this club, a sense of history and tradition. Even the name is beautifully symmetrical, with five letters in each word. **"**

John Gregory waxes lyrical, 1998

66 There is a very good living to be made at Villa Park, provided the club never looks in danger of getting relegated. **99**

Wolverhampton Express & Star reporter
Martin Swain sums up the 'comfort zone' mentality
of Villa during the late-1990s

> **Stress is a player at Rochdale with a family to bring up and a contract expiring at the end of the season.**

John Gregory, commenting on Stan Collymore's admission to the Priory Hospital suffering from stress, 1999

66 I've said to him, "I wish I was you, Stan. I wish I was on the money you're earning. I wish I had your lifestyle. And most of all I wish I had your talent because with it, I'd have been the first name in the England team." **99**

Gregory tries a slightly more conciliatory approach towards his errant forward

❝ You can't be sure he will be taken on by a club anywhere. Unless it's some Outer Mongolian outfit that has been locked away from news, television and society for 10 years. **❞**

The Nottingham Post after a report that Forest were considering taking Collymore off Villa's hands in 1999. They didn't...

> **"** The fans wanted Ginger Spice in basque and suspenders. I gave them Norah Batty in wrinkled stockings. **"**

John Gregory on how he managed his resources

" There are 92 league teams, but whenever a pantomime like this happens, you know who one of the clubs will be. **"**

A *Heroes & Villains* fanzine editorial during one of Villa's many transfer wrangles in the 1990s

" They never cease to think up ways to embarrass you. **"**

Heard from **the crowd** during one of the club's more ludicrous attempts to whip up pre-match fervour as yet another fanfare sounded out to announce the arrival of the teams onto the pitch

> **"** My addictions are always there, waiting there for me. They're doing press-ups outside my door. **"**

Paul Merson, 1999

66 To compete week-in, week-out against the Man Us, Arsenals, Liverpools and Chelseas says a lot about the little team from Birmingham that plays so big! **99**

Programme for a pre-season tournament in New York, 1999

" There's something curious about the relationship between Coventry and Villa. We don't particularly dislike them. But blimey, do they hate us! **"**

John Gregory on the vagaries of West Midlands football, 1999

66 I personally think referees should be wired up to a couple of electrodes and they should be allowed to make three mistakes before you run 50,000 volts through their genitals. **99**

Gregory during his run-ins with referees at the start of the 1999–2000 season

66 Too many of us were playing in the comfort zone, where it doesn't hurt enough if we lost. Sometimes I wonder if we care enough. 99

Paul Merson, talking about Villa's underachieving side of the late-1990s

" Villa always give the impression that they're happier being sixth in the table than second. Because they can get to sixth without much effort, but when they're second they have to try to be first. "

Holy Trinity fanzine editor **Steve Whitehouse** expands on the 'comfort zone' mentality

66 There's as much chance of a recession as there is of Aston Villa winning the league. **99**

Villa fan **Mervyn King** on being appointed Governor of the Bank of England in 1999. Villa were top of the league at the time...

66 Why all the fuss over Prince William becoming an Aston Villa fan? At least he didn't choose to support Manchester United like everybody else in Berkshire. 99

Sun columnist **Richard Littlejohn**, 2000

" Carbone retired with the dignity of a three-year-old being led past the sweet counter at Tesco, flinging down his headband and kicking the trainer's bucket. **"**

The *Guardian's* **David Lacey** on Benito Carbone's histrionics during the 2000 FA Cup semi-final versus Bolton

" That man Boateng must have an incredibly hard chin. **"**

Paul Gascoigne's agent, **Mel Stein**,
after his player broke an arm on
George Boateng's face, 2000

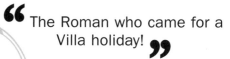

" The Roman who came for a Villa holiday! **"**

A sardonic description of **Gustavo Bartelt** whose loan spell from Roma was less than successful, 2000

" I'm a much better manager than when I started, but not half as good as I will be. **"**

John Gregory's mission statement, 2000

66 It was beautiful. The sensitivity from everyone he met in Birmingham really impressed David. **99**

Chantelle Stanley, David Ginola's agent, shortly after the French winger signed for Villa in 2000

❝ You wonder if this city will ever run out of grey paint. **❞**

David Ginola didn't take long to be less than
impressed with Birmingham

" Young Gareth Barry, you know, he's young. **"**

The ever-astute **Kevin Keegan** on the qualities of
Gareth Barry

" Aston Villa always seem to have problems taking the final step towards being a really big club. **"**

Graham Taylor on his return to Villa Park as
manager of Watford in 2001

" I was in hospital with instructions not to have any visitors for 24 hours. I awoke to find Ron Atkinson at the end of my bed saying, "Sorry, I'm late, but I had to walk round the hospital three times before anybody recognised me." "

TV presenter **Gary Newbon**

> **"** The ever-growing number of spokesmen, for the ever-growing number of Villa protest groups. **"**

Martin Swain's sardonic look at the unique nature of Villa supporter politics, February 2002

" I think they're great. **"**

His Royal Highness **Prince William**
on Aston Villa

" I have reached an agreement with an English club, but I cannot say the club's name. Aston Villa know the club's name. I will play for the biggest club in England. **"**

Alpay Ozalan, speaking in January 2003 – eight months before Villa cancelled his contract. Alpay's current whereabouts are unknown…

" I know almost every player by name already. I play a lot of Championship Manager and Gareth Barry is always a good buy. Hopefully he is just as good in real life. **"**

Joey Gudjonsson on signing for Villa in January 2003

> **"** All around I see hope fading.
> And you ask any football fan –
> a life without hope is a life not
> worth living. **"**

Local historian and Villa supporter **Carl Chinn** in an
interview with *The Times*, March 2003

> **"** The vast majority of Mr Gregory's transfer dealings were unfortunate. A vast fortune in transfer fees and wages were committed to players who in the main did not match up to expectations. **"**

The Hodgson Report into the business workings of Aston Villa, summer 2003

" There are fundamental problems at Aston Villa that are preventing it from becoming a top four club. **"**

Graham Taylor upon resigning as manager, 2003

66 There is certainly more interest in (the political) side of things from the media than I expected. 99

David O'Leary soon learned that managing the Villa was no ordinary job, 2003

❝ One thing I took this job for was to prove that David O'Leary doesn't need money. **❞**

O'Leary who also quickly learned realism,
Villa Park-style

" Ten worst examples of footballers behaving badly. Number 7 – Dwight Yorke (with guest appearance from Mark Bosnich), 1998. Vital ingredients: Four girls, a hidden video, dressing up in women's clothing. **"**

The Observer Sport Monthly, 2003

> **"** Lee Hendrie is Lee Hendrie and he will always be Lee Hendrie. **"**

David O'Leary in 2004, endorsing the view that genetic engineering can only progress so far

> **"** O'Leary was never anything less than courteous, friendly and, above all, professional. But he did appear to have a secretive, cynical, perhaps spiteful, side to his nature. **"**

Leeds supporter **Gary Edwards**, writing about David O'Leary's time at Elland Road

" What's it like to make a sub? "

Leeds supporters' chant aimed at O'Leary on his
return there as Villa manager, 2003–04, a
comment on his reluctance to make changes
during a game

66 Finest Hour: marrying on the pitch. It made *Match of the Day*. 99

Villa mascot **Bella**, when she and fellow furry creature, Hercules the Lion, got married and the ceremony was shown on national TV

" I do know her through a friend but I'm not giving her one. **"**

The ever-gallant **Lee Hendrie** on his relationship with *Big Brother's* Jade Goody

> **"** His name is Angel,
> And he's a show boy.
> An Alice band keeps up his hair:
> Juan Pablo from Col-om-biare. **"**

The opening lines of a poem that won Birmingham City
supporter **Jonny Hurst** the title of Barclaycard
Premiership Poet Laureate

> **"** With my Jamaican hand on
>   my Ethiopian heart,
> The African heart deep in
>   my Brummie chest.
> And I chant, Aston Villa,
> Aston Villa, Aston Villa…
> I don't have an identity crisis. **"**

From "Knowing Me" by Rastafarian Brummie poet
Benjamin Zephaniah

> **"** I'm big on Aston Villa because the name is just so sweet. Other clubs are like "Arrrrsenal" or "Maaaan United" but Aston Villa sounds like a lovely spa. **"**

Film star **Tom Hanks** explaining why he's a Villa supporter, 2004

> **"** Le rock d'Aston Villa se porte toujours aussi bien après une Victoire de la Musique et quelques changements de personnel. **"**

From a review of French band **Aston Villa**'s album *Strange*

66 As a boy, I found that the exotic Englishness of such names oddly resembled those of Crystal Palace, Aston Villa, West Bromwich Albion and Charlton Athletic – all more exciting than the Knights of the Round Table in their silly tin armour, by far. 99

Poet and author **Chris Wallace-Crabbe** from Australian newspaper *The Age*, 2004

The few trees through the corner gap are beginning to green and beyond them the M6, the world of nowhere, the world of coming from and going to, a perpetual conveyor belt.

From "The Team in My Head" by poet and Villa fan
David Harte

" I promised you in 1969 that no one person or group of people would ever be allowed to control the club... I have never had a controlling shareholding in Aston Villa and have no wish to do so. **"**

Doug Ellis, when fighting unsuccessfully to retain his seat on the board in 1979

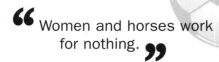

“ Women and horses work for nothing. **”**

Deadly Doug on voting himself another pay rise

66 When he was recovering in hospital, one of our sons said the words, "Doug Ellis", and the heart monitor went shooting up. All the nurses came rushing in. **99**

Rosina Barton, wife of former Villa manager Tony, describes her husband's recovery from a heart attack in 1984

" Hands up if you know this man. **"**

Doug Ellis to the assembled media corps when
introducing new manager Dr Josef Venglos
in 1990

❝ It was a total surprise. I was gobsmacked. **❞**

Doug Ellis describes his response to hearing that Villa Park's new stand was to be named after him as a 70th birthday present, January 1994

" Ron Atkinson is one of the top three managers in the country. **"**

Ellis again, November 1994. Big Ron was sacked
five days later

" I will never sack another manager. "

Doug Ellis in prophetic mood, 1997. Since then, three Villa managers have resigned

❝ Ask him about his
bleeding shares. **❞**

Comment from a **Villa supporter** to author David
Conn, who had mentioned that he was off to
interview Ellis shortly after the club floated on
the Stock Exchange in 1997

> **My trouble is that I'm a devil for seeing the other fellow's point of view.**

A philosophical **Doug Ellis** in an interview with the
Irish Sunday Tribune, 1998

66 Mr Ellis, you have presided over the destruction of the Trinity Road stand, the finest site in English football. Your penny-pinching has presided over the destruction of the team and the share price. Most people would be expected to fall on their sword and I urge everyone to vote against this resolution. **99**

Villa shareholder **Peter Warillow** at the club's AGM, September 2000. Doug Ellis was kicked off the board on a show of hands but reinstated three days later after utilising his block vote

> The trouble is that the chairman thinks we're like Manchester United, but acts small. We have to put up with that. He thinks we're the only club in the area, and that everybody has to support Aston Villa. He's stuck in a time warp. We're dragging him, kicking and screaming, into the millennium.

John Gregory provokes the Wrath of Ellis, December 2000

" This is my life. I kick every ball and sign every cheque. They'll carry me out of here in a box. "

Doug Ellis issues a promise, or maybe a threat

" I'm a frustrated, would-be professional player who in the end wasn't good enough. **"**

A rare admission of failure from **Doug Ellis**, 2000

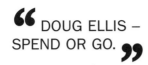

**" DOUG ELLIS –
SPEND OR GO. "**

The wording of a **poster campaign** that mysteriously
sprang up around the West Midlands, December
2000. He did neither

" It's nothing personal. "

Ian Robinson, who stood as a candidate in the 2001 general election as an Ellis Out candidate for the Sutton Coldfield constituency where Doug Ellis lives

66 I'm pretty certain that Villa will be under new ownership by the start of next season. **99**

Contributor to Villa website *Villatalk*, July 2003, when Venezuelan billionaire Gustavo Cisernos was linked with a takeover of the club. Doug stayed

66 Going up against you at this meeting, Mr Ellis, is like farting against thunder. **99**

Shareholder **Peter Page** during yet another AGM debate on Doug Ellis's chairmanship, 2004

66 I play a bit of snooker myself and I watch quite a lot, but that isn't why I was named as I am. Unfortunately I've never met Steve Davis, the snooker player, I've only seen him on TV. **99**

Steven Davies *on his cue-wielding namesake*

❝ Strikers wanted. **❞**

Written on a whiteboard at **Villa's training ground** at the end of 2004–05, when the side managed just 45 league goals

“ I'm just sad. But you move on with life and I just wish Aston Villa all the very best. **”**

David O'Leary leaves Villa, July 2006

> **I realise expectations are pretty high. I'm petrified! It's a great challenge and I'm raring to go but I have to prove myself and show I can do the job.**

Martin O'Neill takes over at the Villa, August 2006

66 Everybody is well aware of the history of the club and while trying to restore it to those glory days is a long way away, why not try? It's a quarter of a century since they won the European Cup and that's a long way away at this minute. 99

O'Neill recognises the scale of the task ahead

66 As a kid you want to play every minute of every game – that's what you dream about. **99**

Gabriel Agbonlahor

“ I've suffered with the "Ellis Out" many times. People think that I've not put anything into it. I can tell you many situations when I've put money and many other things into it. **”**

Doug Ellis, three months after stepping down from his post as Villa chairman

" O'Neill is the saviour of this club, not me. You don't meddle with the top guys or they won't work for you. You can't get the best if you spend all day poking them in the ribs. **"**

New owner **Randy Lerner** promises not to interfere in team matters

" Martin O'Neill is a legend. You never hear a player say a bad word about him – even when they are not in the team. You feel like he wants to know the players as well as he can and he knows how to help each player. **"**

Stiliyan Petrov

❝ You could be looking at him becoming one of Villa's great players. He's already played over 300 games and he's only 25. **❞**

O'Neill on skipper Gareth Barry

❝ I want a life of good sport, good people and the competition that goes with it. I'm here to try to get something accomplished. **❞**

New Villa owner **Randy Lerner** on his motivation

For someone who is so tall, he has got a great touch and, make no mistake, he can definitely play.

Martin O'Neill on John Carew

66 This could be the last big move I make in my career, so I want to make the most of it. 99

John Carew, formerly of Valencia, Roma and Olympique Lyonnais, January 2007

" The fee doesn't worry me. The manager agreed that fee with Watford. He has put his faith in me, he is very ambitious, and so am I. **"**

Ashley Young is unfazed by his £8 million price tag, January 2007

" When he let me go, I wanted to prove I could really play. The next five years, whenever Villa played United, we walked past each other. Then, after we beat United in the 1994 League Cup Final, Alex put his hand out and said, "Well done, big man." It made me wish I had gone up to him first. **"**

Paul McGrath experiences Alex Ferguson's magnanimous side

66 I'm still claret and blue through and through. I'm just desperate for us to win. 99

Former Villa supremo **Doug Ellis**

66 The once-crumbling Holte Hotel, as much a symbol of Randy Lerner's Villa as the decay and dereliction of the place in the last days of the previous regime. **99**

Author and Villa supporter **Stephen Pennell**, in his book *Star Spangled Villans*

" When you get down in the mud and wrestle with a pig, the pig loves it – and you get muddy. **"**

Villa director **General Charles Krulak**, commenting on his alleged fallout with Birmingham City director David Gold

66 There are still Villa fans who
thank me for what I did there. **99**

David O'Leary, former Villa manager and possibly
the most deluded man in football

" We aim to be like Aston Villa. "

Newcastle chief executive **Derek Llambias**,
February 2009

"Who's your next messiah – Ant or Dec?"

Holte End banner versus Newcastle, last day of the 2008–09 season. Villa won, United were relegated

" I am happy here. There is speculation that players are going to clubs all the time but I am happy here. Since the first day I came here I have enjoyed every minute. **"**

Villa midfielder **Stewart Downing**, April 2011. He left three months later

66 That was rubbish – I looked like a pub player. **99**

Defender **Curtis Davies** after his debut

66 I was on the terraces for the Villa v Tranmere League Cup semi-final game. We were 3–1 down and pulled it back in the match at Villa Park. For years, I was a fan singing on the terraces. Now supporters are singing to me while I play. That's massive. 99

Villa player **Craig Gardner**, 2008

❝ I've always been a Blues fan. **❞**

Birmingham City player **Craig Gardner**, 2010

" I was most upset when people started saying "Why does Private Pike support West Ham?" He doesn't! It's Aston Villa – always was, always will be and still is. "

Dad's Army star and Villa supporter **Ian Lavender**

66 There were times when he resembled a misty-eyed pensioner on a nostalgic coach tour of day trips to favourite haunts from his Premier League past. **99**

Birmingham Mail reporter **Matt Kendrick**, talking about the recently departed Gerard Houllier, May 2011

" Anyone who got Birmingham relegated twice in the space of four years should be seen as something of a cult hero at Villa Park. **"**

Daily Telegraph reporter **Sandy Macaskill** when Alex McLeish was appointed Villa manager, June 2011

66 I am honoured to have this opportunity to manage a club with such a fantastic history as Aston Villa's. The heritage, the history of success and the tradition of Aston Villa are compelling and irresistible. The challenge for me is to try to add my own chapter. **99**

Alex McLeish June 2011

"It's our year for the FA Cup. "

Every Villa supporter, every January